Trill Studies for the Cello

Book One: Preparatory Exercises

by Cassia Harvey

CHP113

©2011 by C. Harvey Publications® All Rights Reserved.
www.charveypublications.com - print books & free sheet music blog
www.learnstrings.com - downloadable books & chamber music

Trill Studies for the Cello, Book One
Practice Suggestions

1. Curve the fingers of the left hand. Play on the tips of the fingers.

2. Start slowly and then increase the speed when the exercise is in tune.

3. Try to go a little faster each day, working to improve your speed from the day before.

4. Keep the shoulder, arm, hand, and fingers relaxed. Make sure the left-hand thumb is loose.

5. Balance the hand over the fingers that are playing.

6. Keep the main weight of the hand on the finger that is held down.
   The trilling finger should feel as free as possible, with the natural weight of the finger doing most of the tapping work.

7. Use a metronome to keep track of your progress at trilling faster.

8. Make sure the sound is clear at every speed.

1

Trill Studies for the Cello, Book One

Trill Studies for the Cello, Book One

2

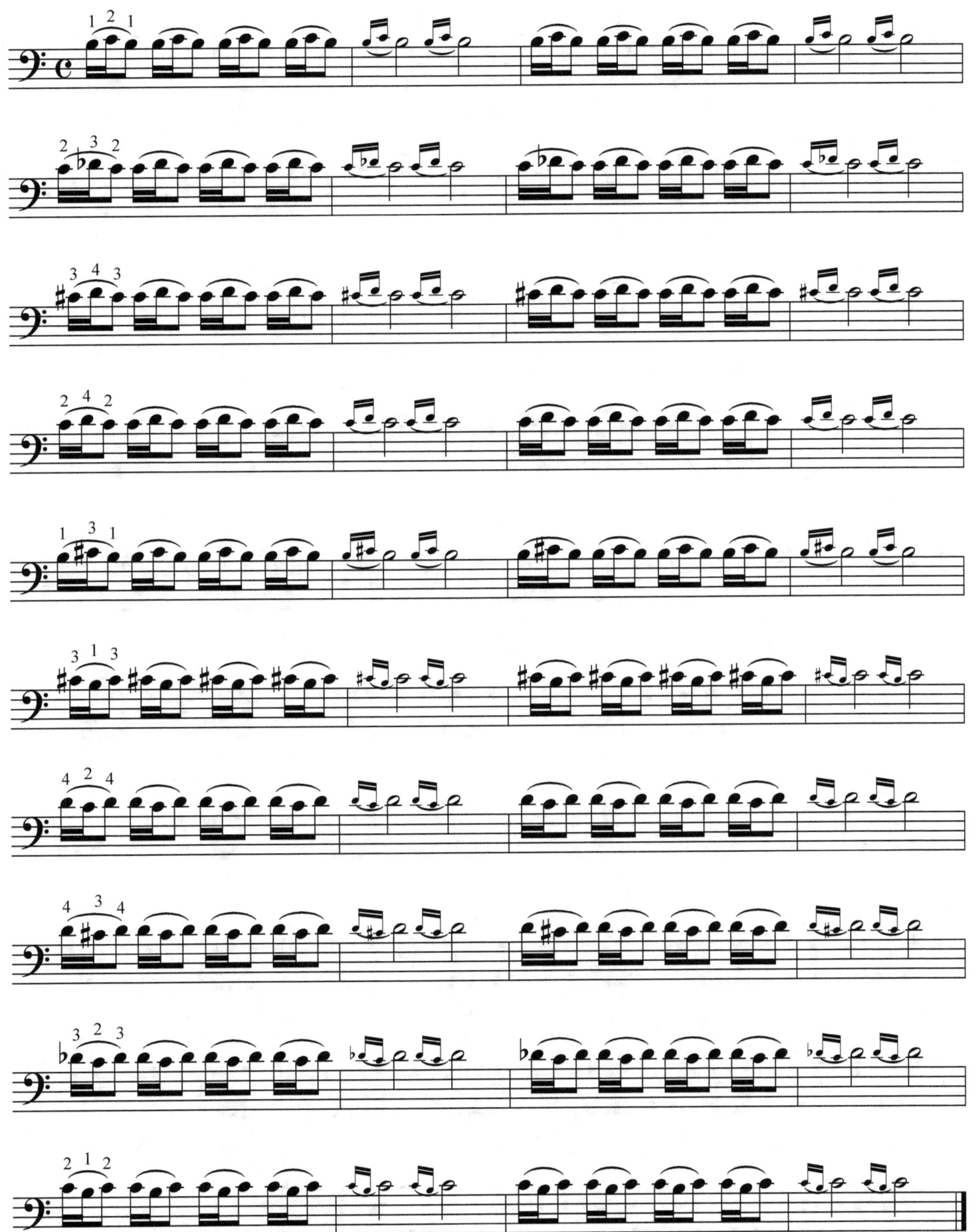

©2011 C. Harvey Publications All Rights Reserved.

3

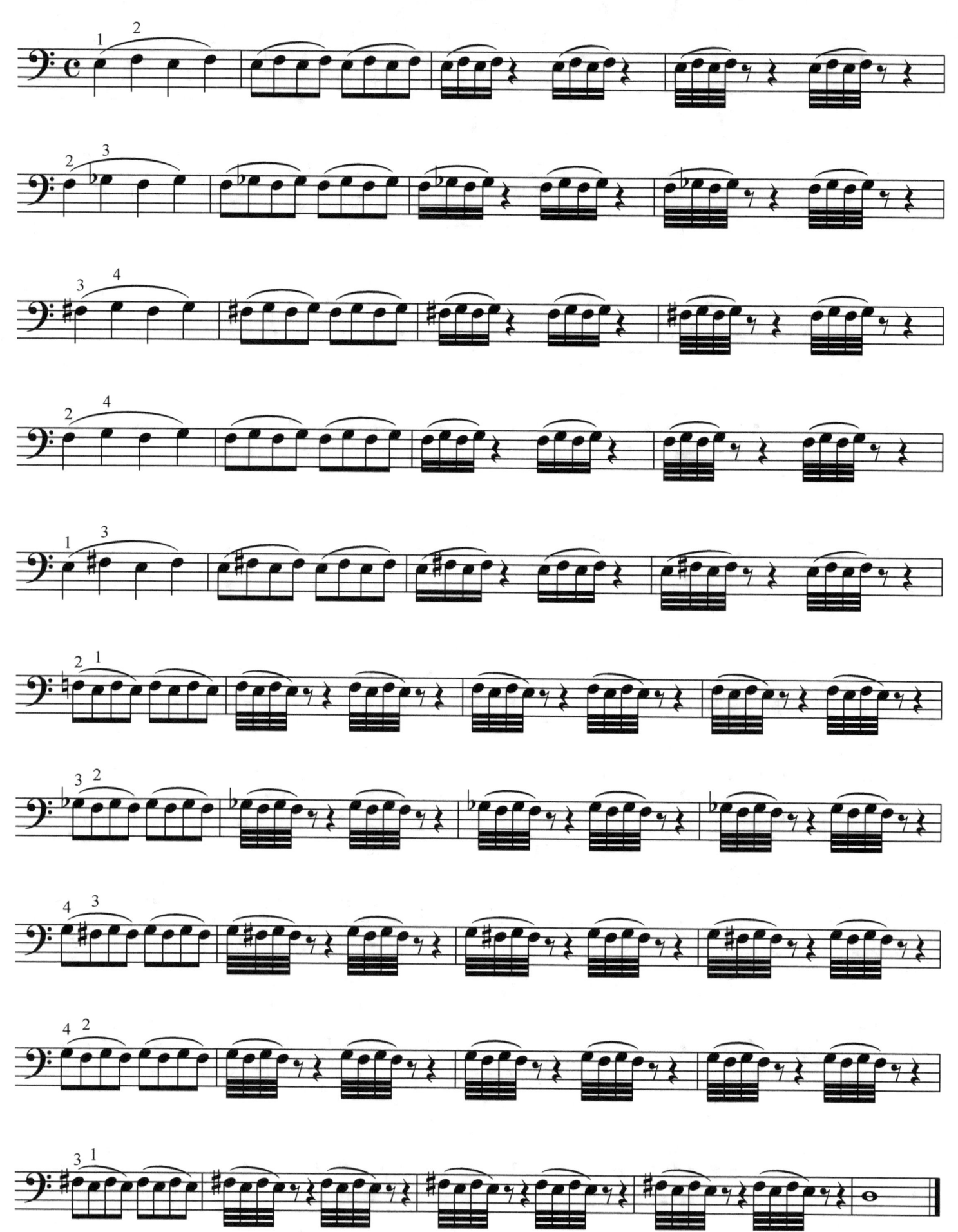

Trill Studies for the Cello, Book One

©2011 C. Harvey Publications All Rights Reserved.

4

5

Trill Studies for the Cello, Book One

©2011 C. Harvey Publications All Rights Reserved.

Trill Studies for the Cello, Book One

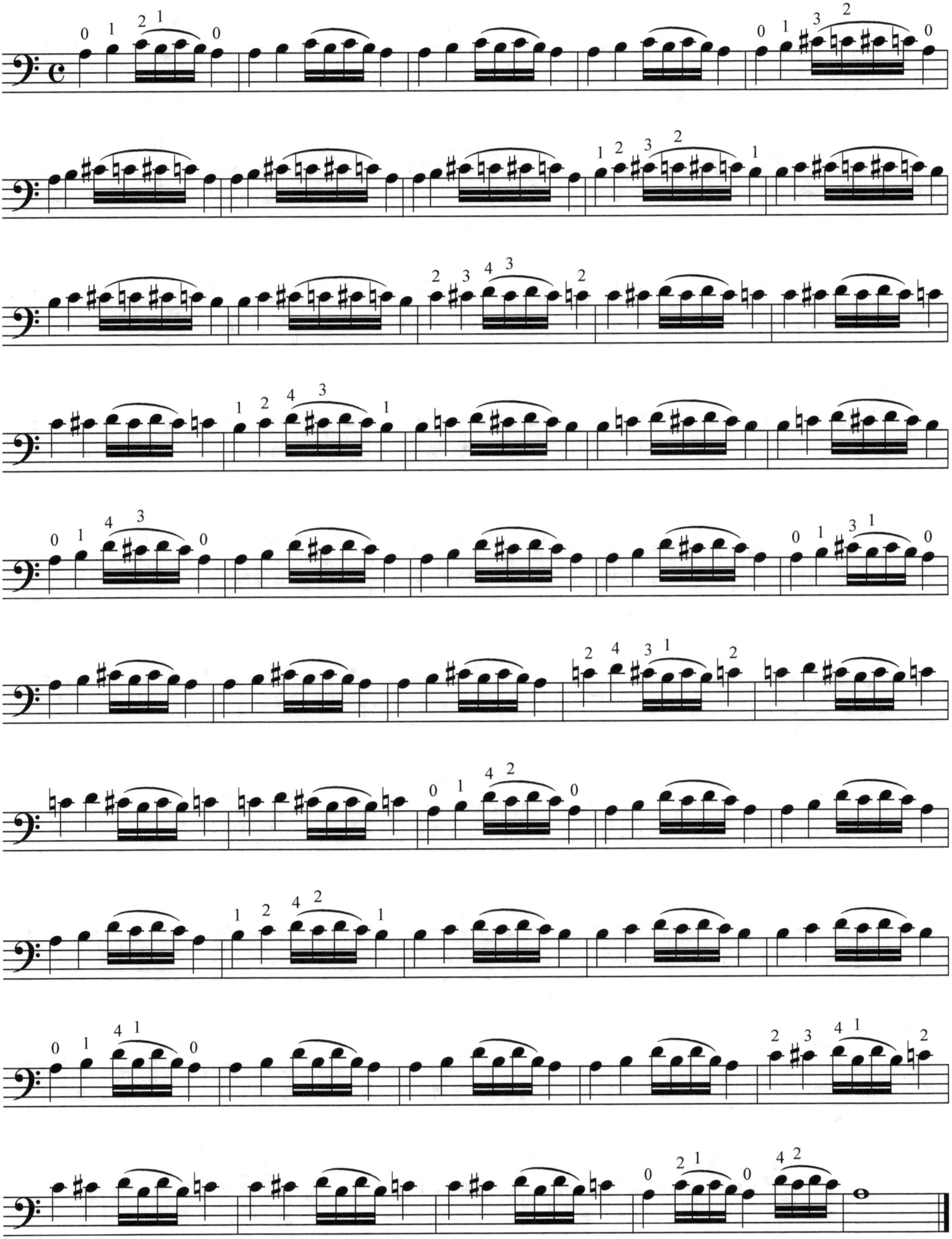

6

7

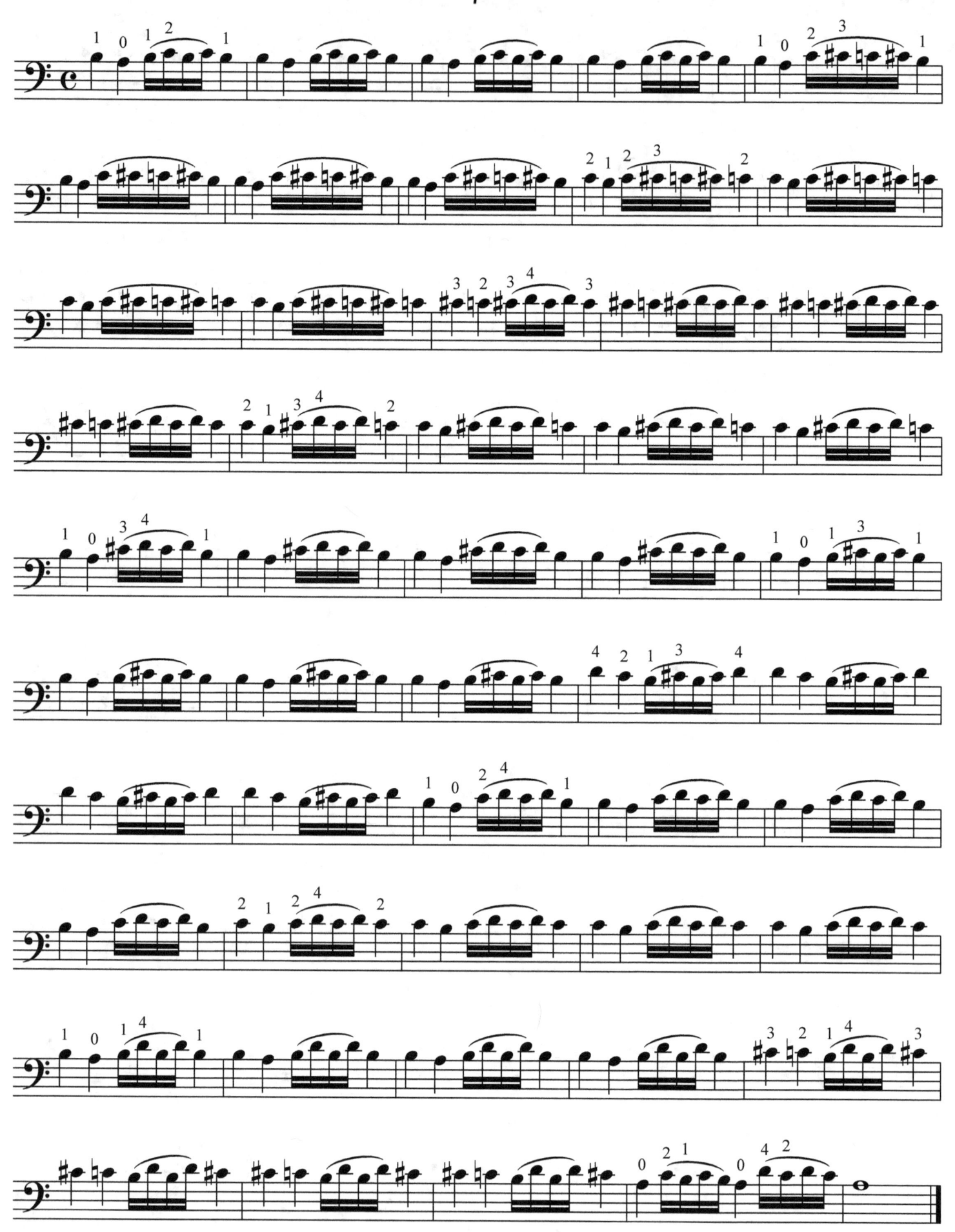

Trill Studies for the Cello, Book One

8

©2011 C. Harvey Publications All Rights Reserved.

9

Trill Studies for the Cello, Book One

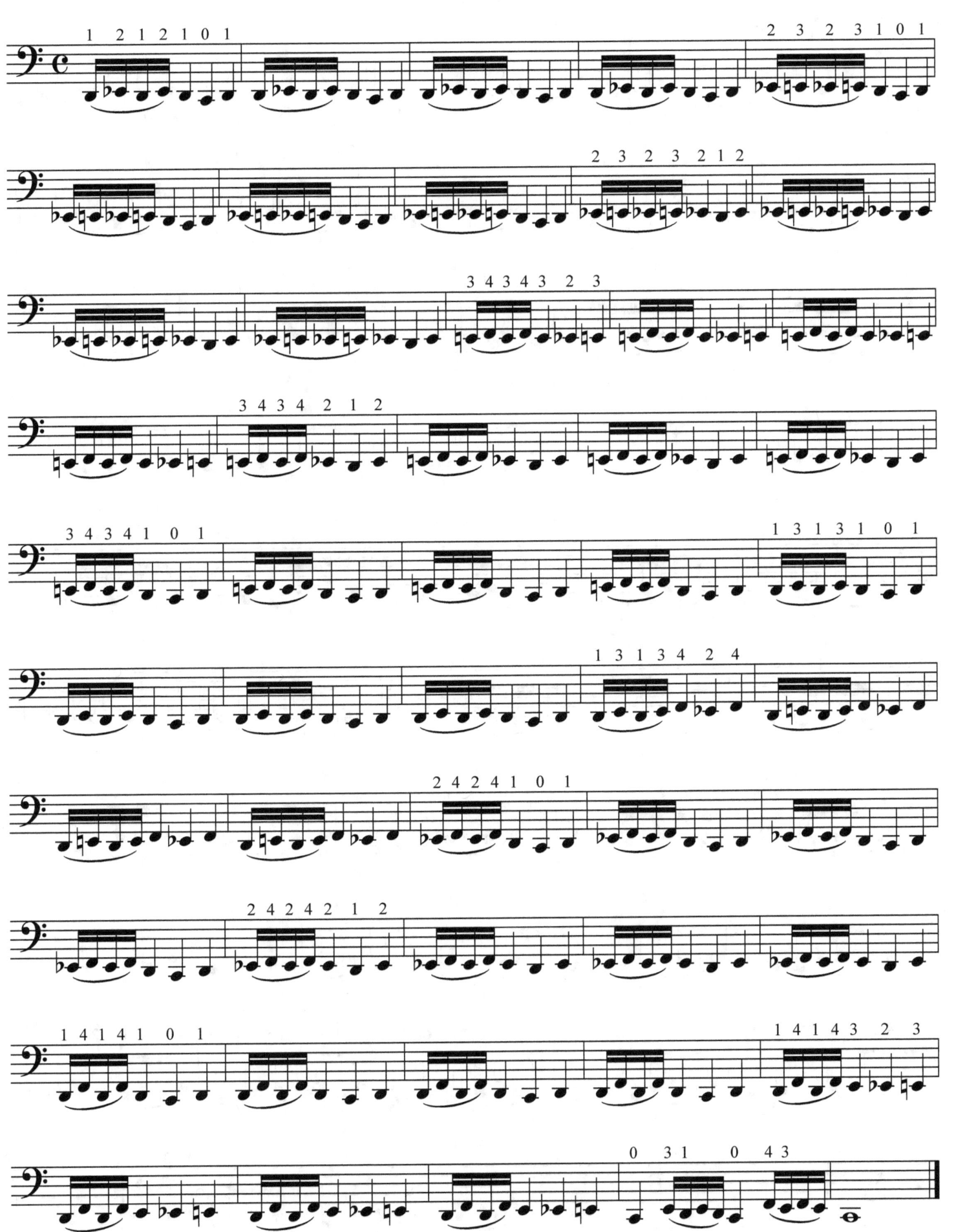

11

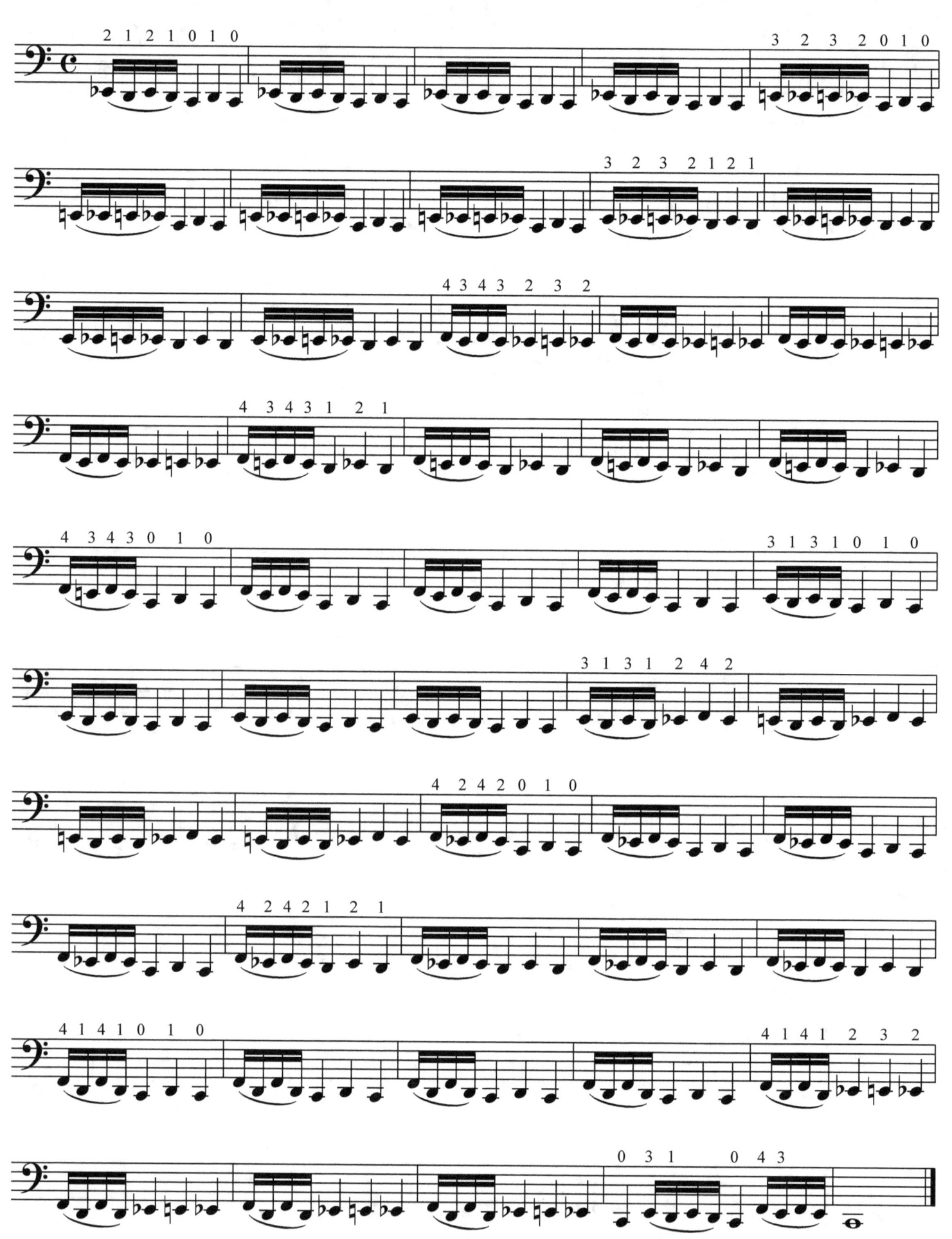

Trill Studies for the Cello, Book One

Trill Studies for the Cello, Book One

12

©2011 C. Harvey Publications All Rights Reserved.

13

Trill Studies for the Cello, Book One

Trill Studies for the Cello, Book One

14

©2011 C. Harvey Publications All Rights Reserved.

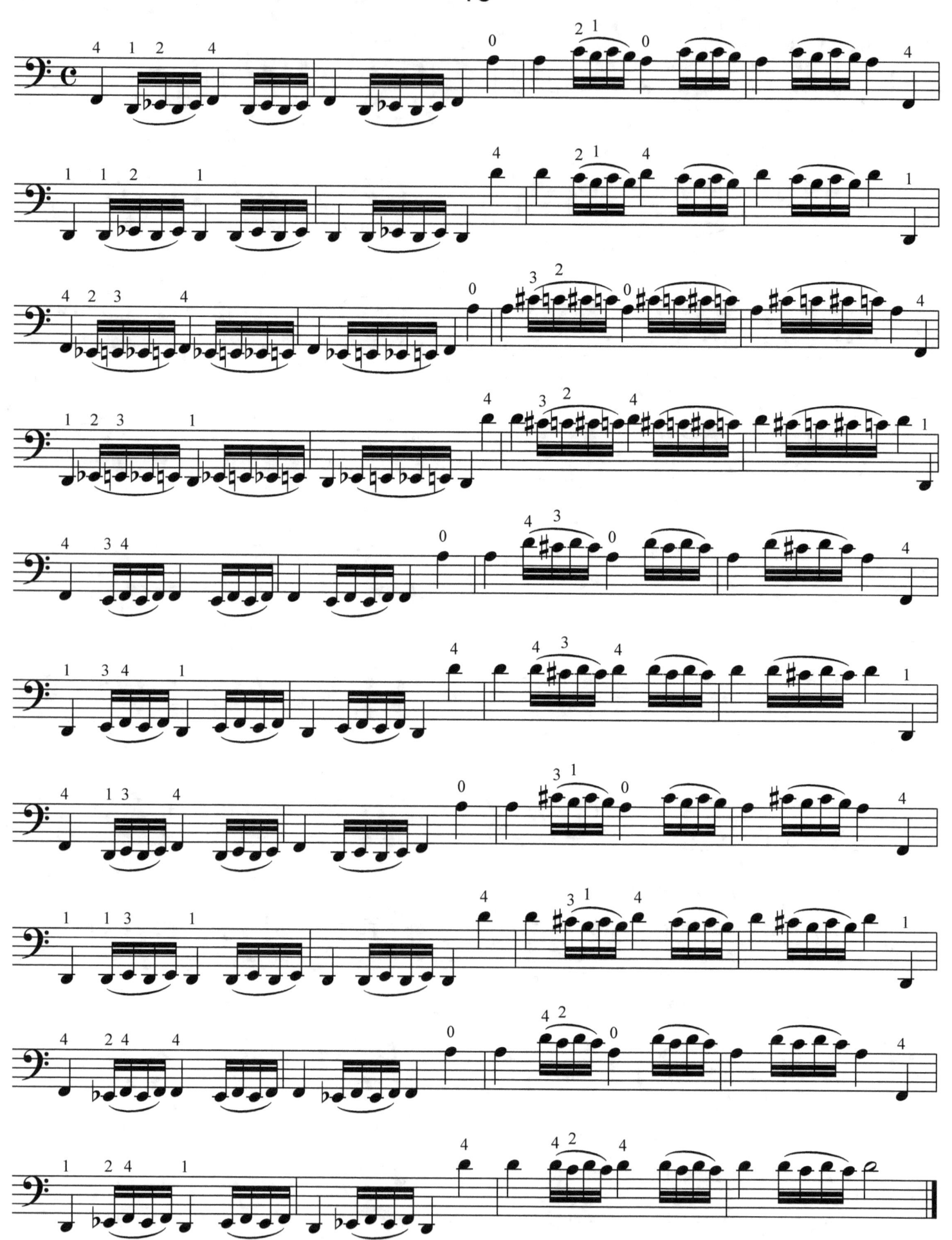

16

17

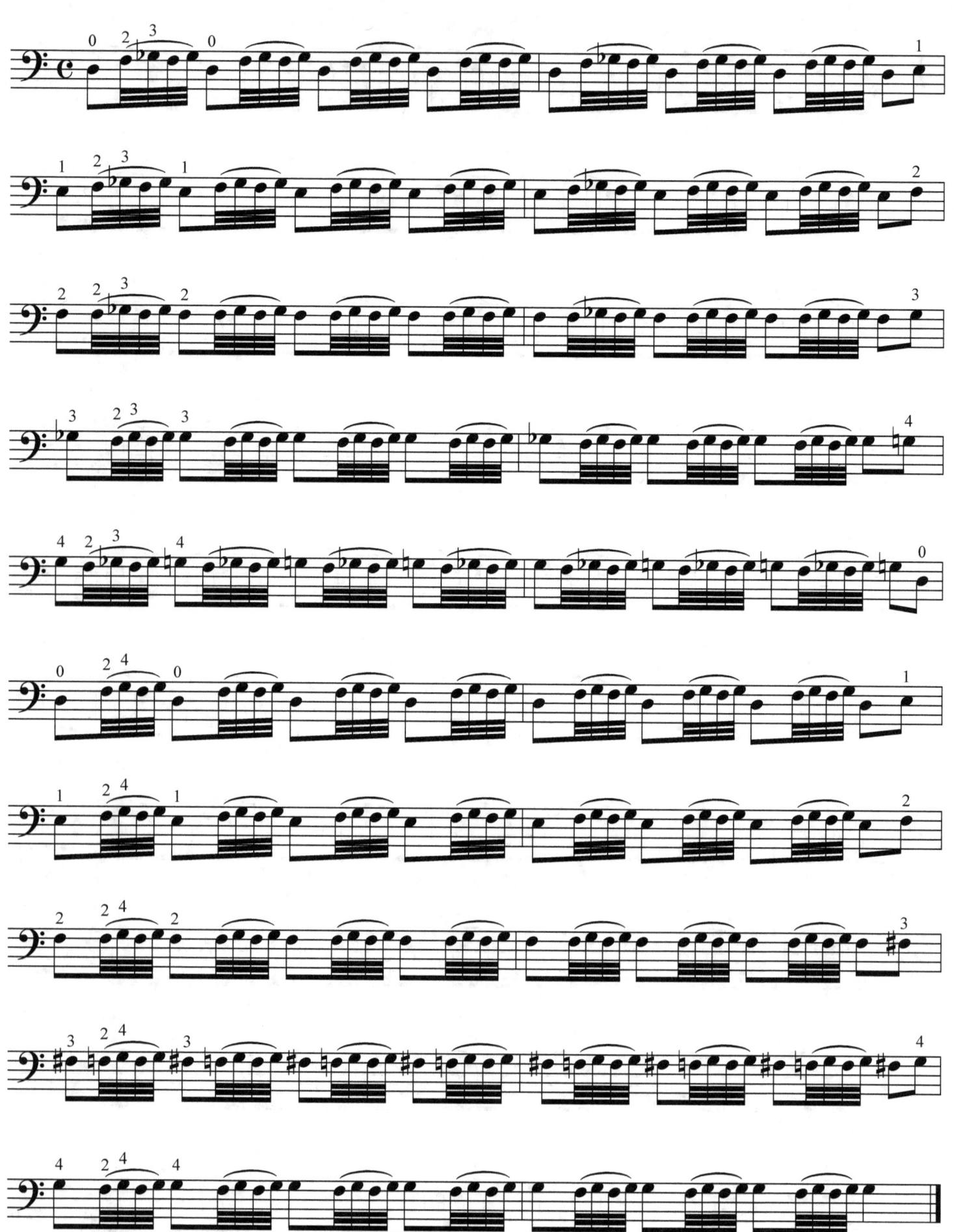

Trill Studies for the Cello, Book One

18

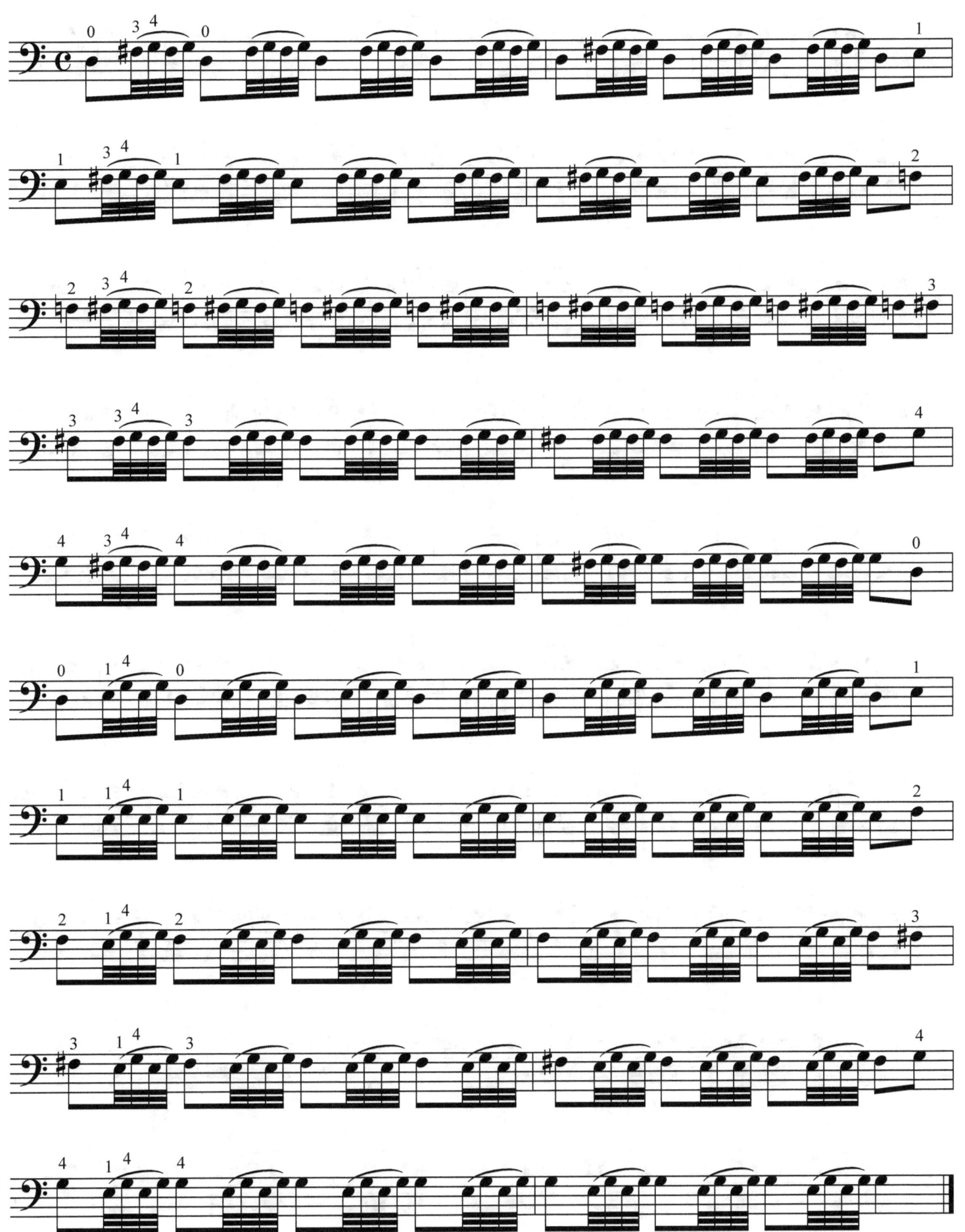

©2011 C. Harvey Publications All Rights Reserved.

19

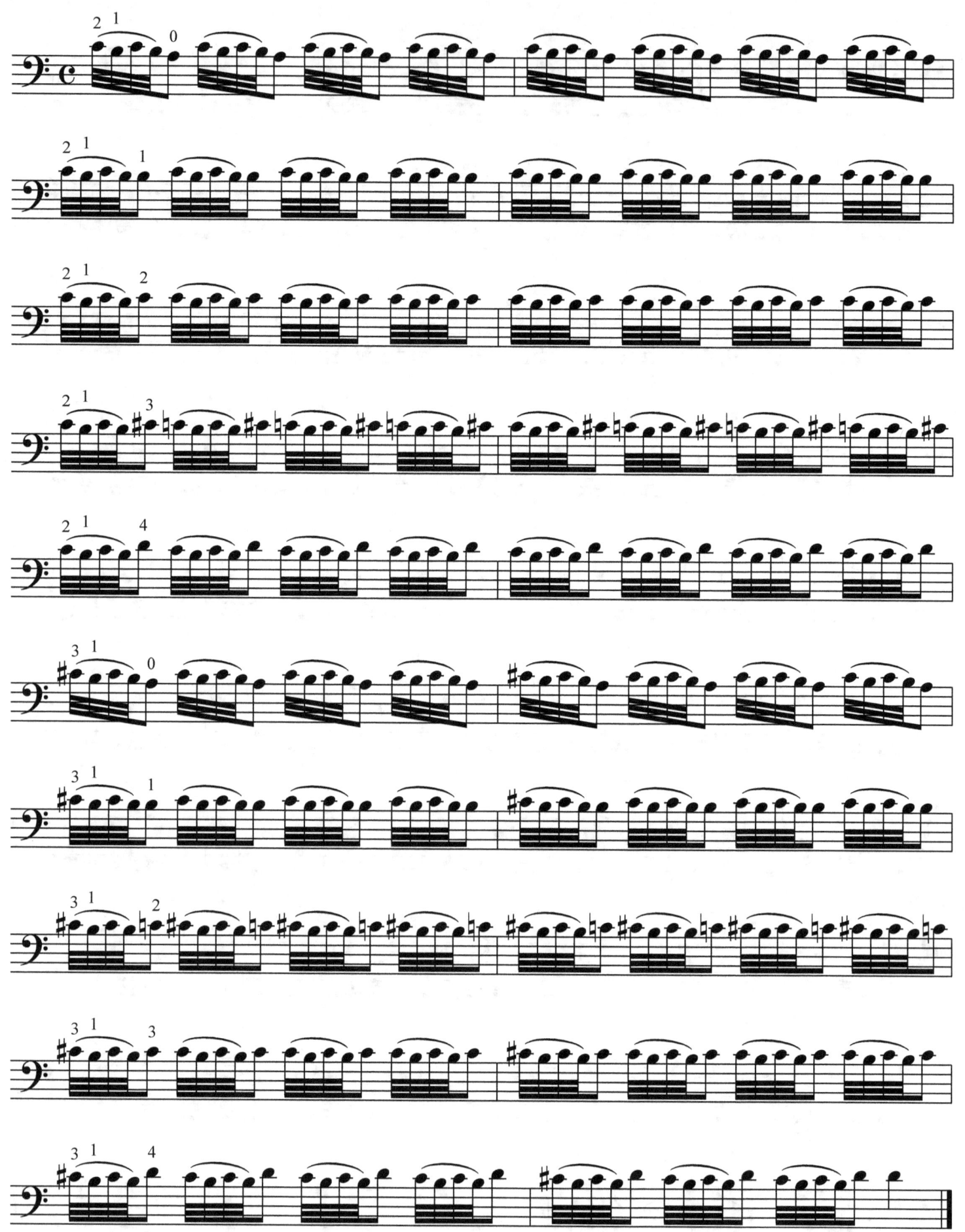

20

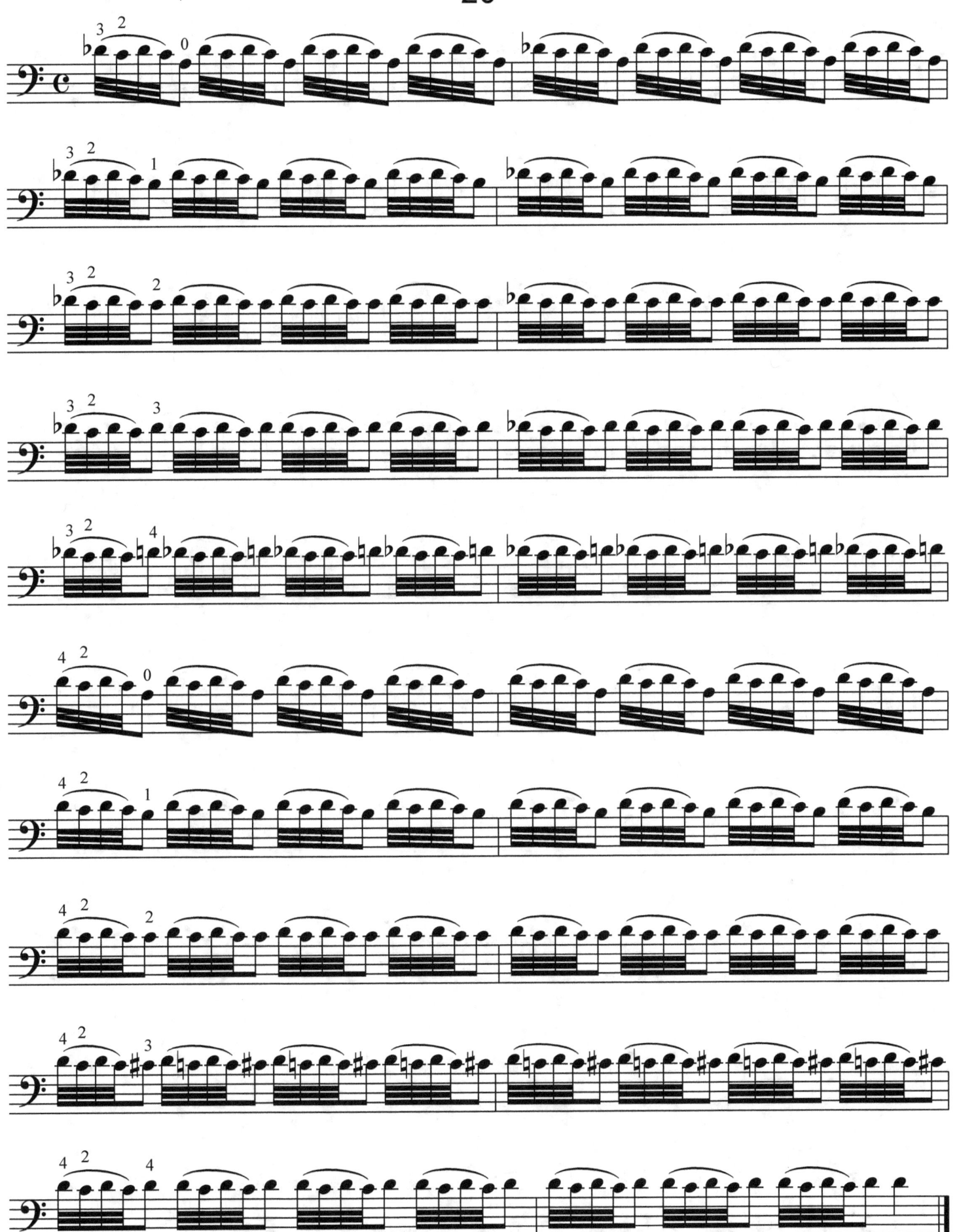

21

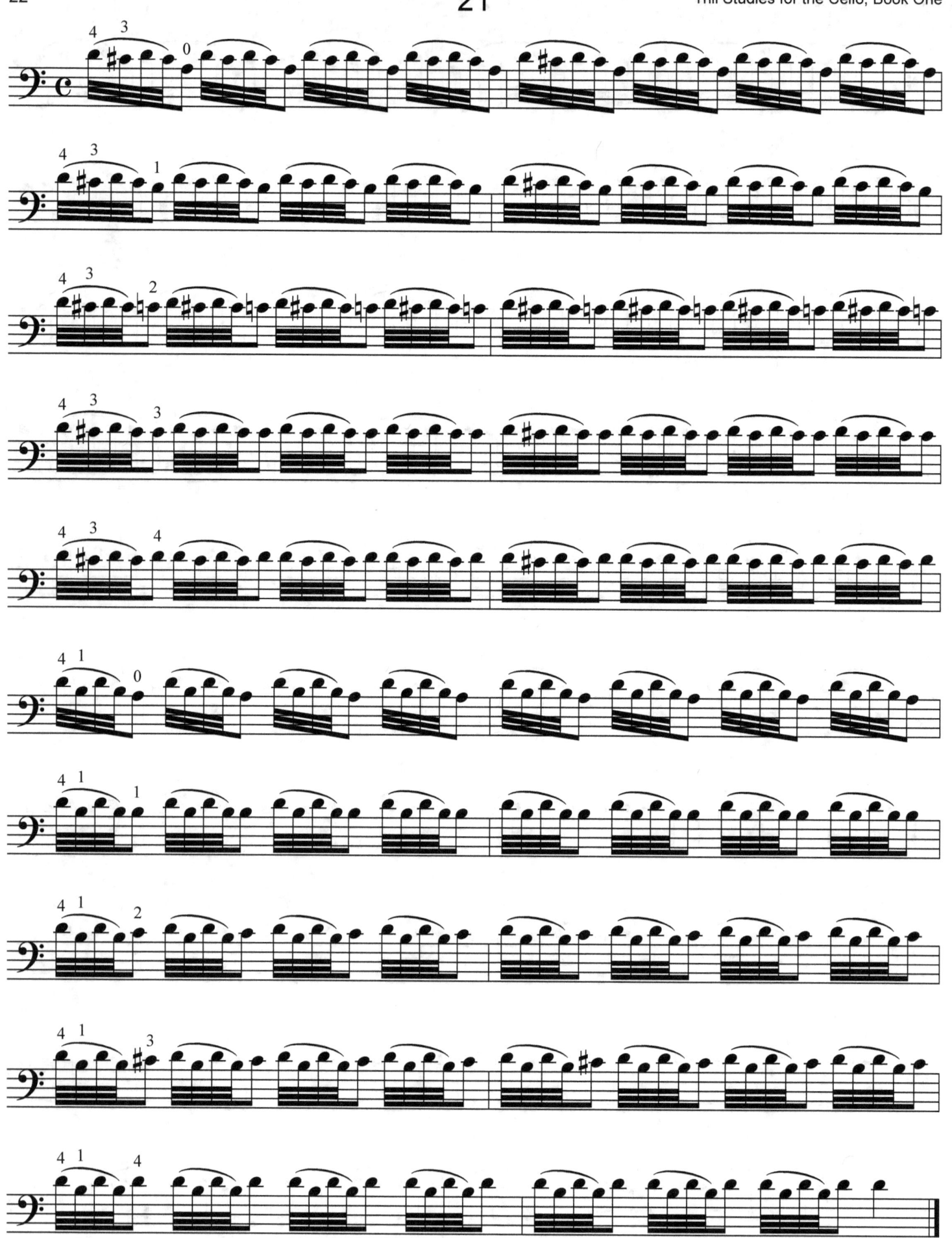

Trill Studies for the Cello, Book One

22

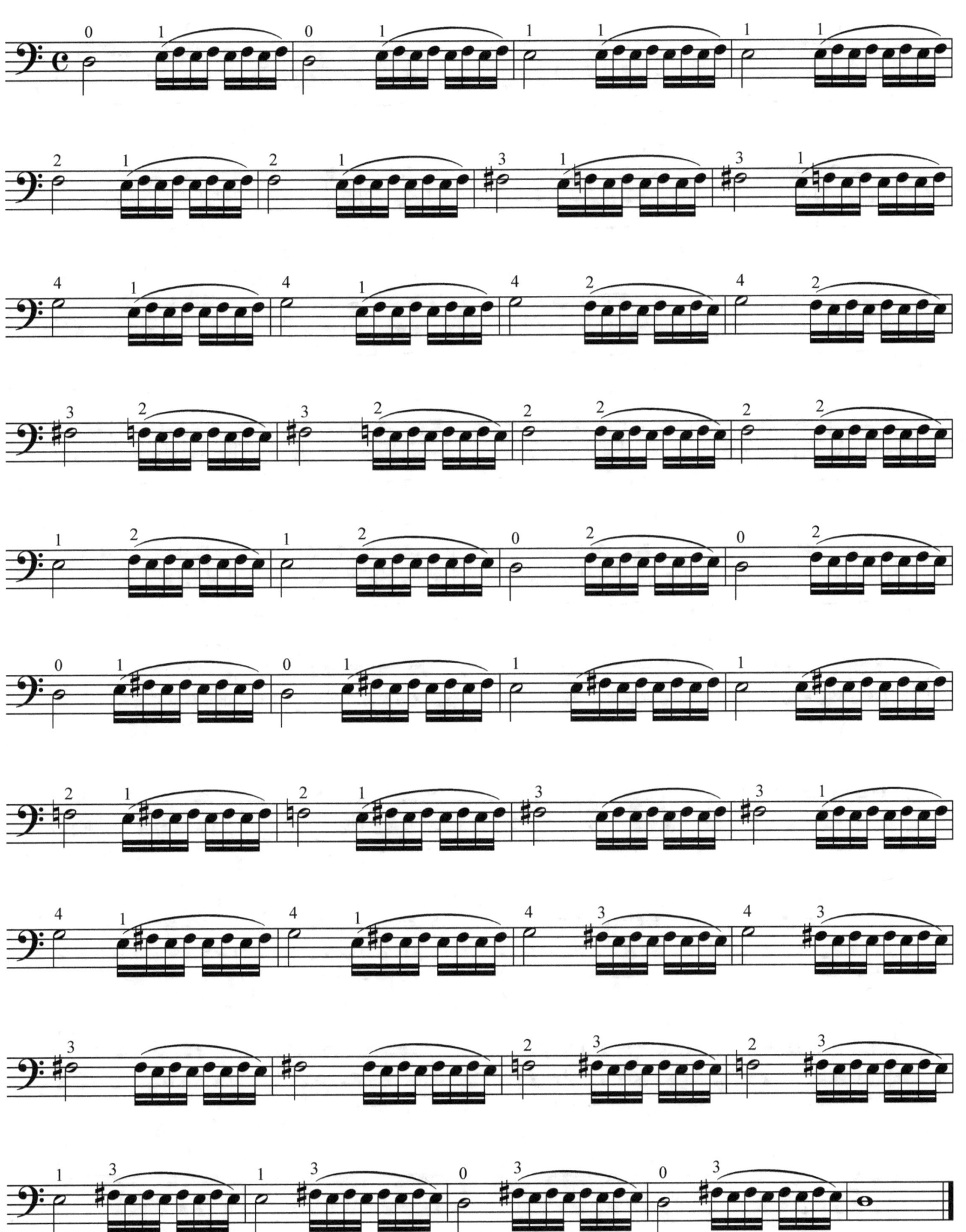

23

Trill Studies for the Cello, Book One

24

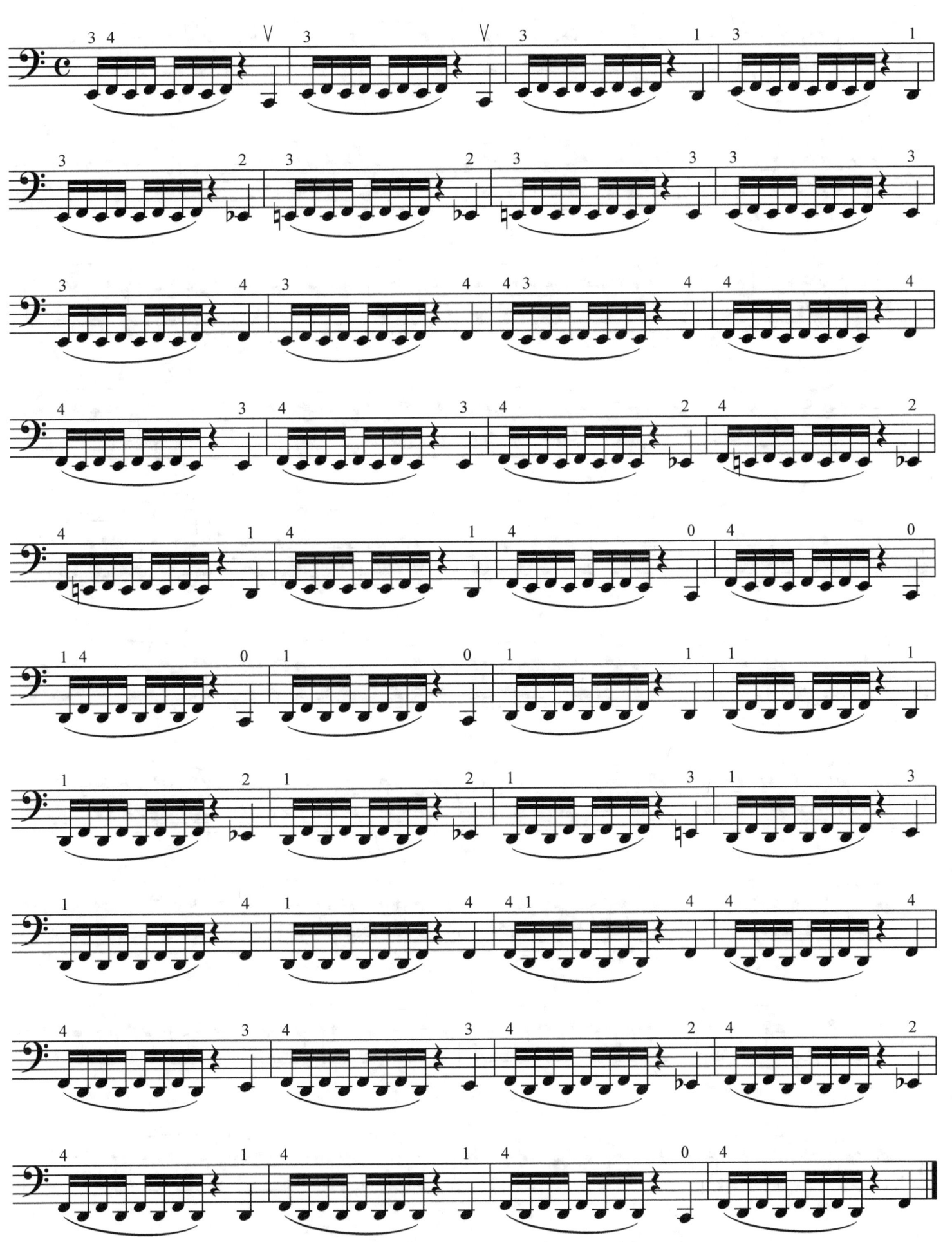

25

Trill Studies for the Cello, Book One

26

Trill Studies for the Cello, Book One

28

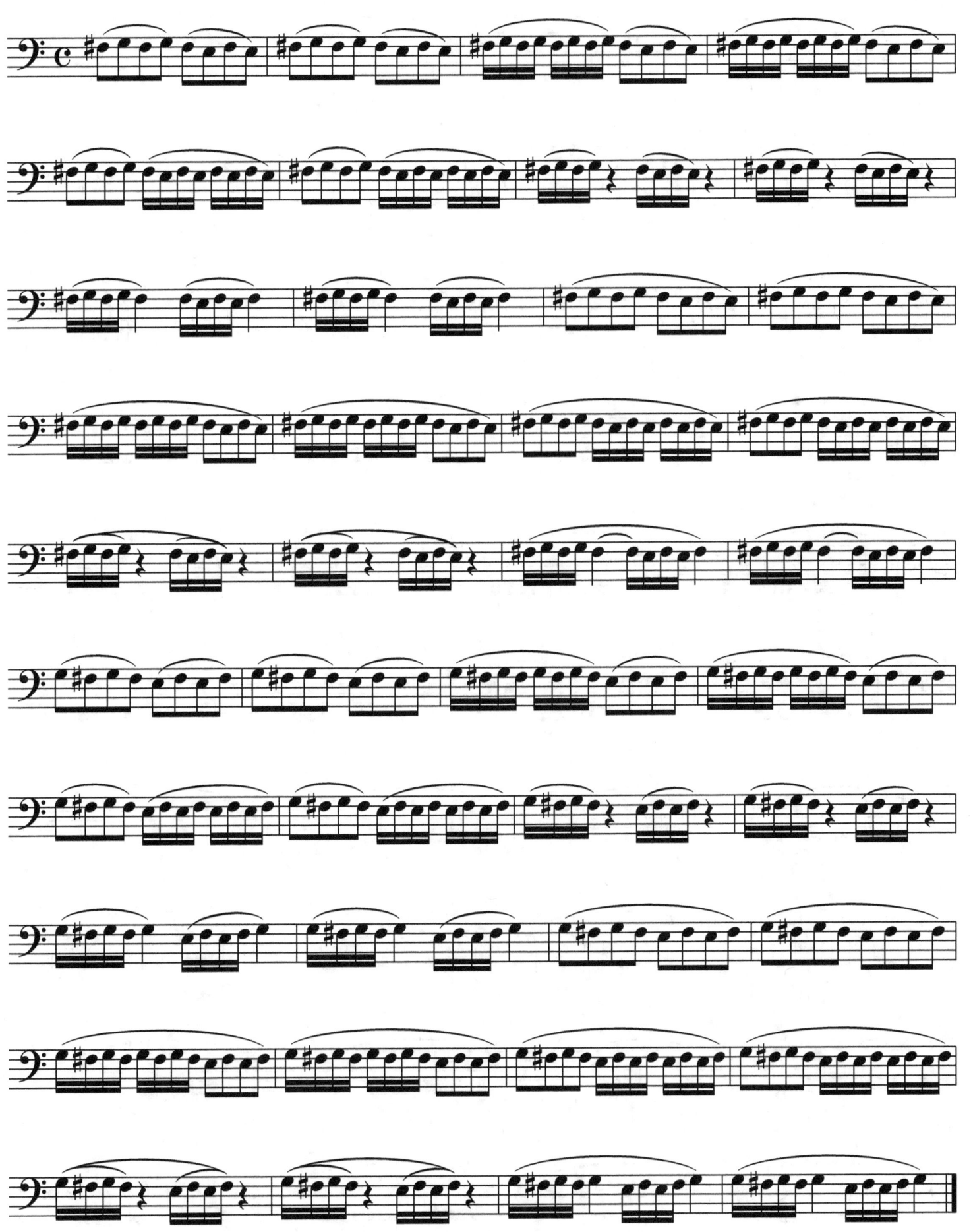

29

Trill Studies for the Cello, Book One

30

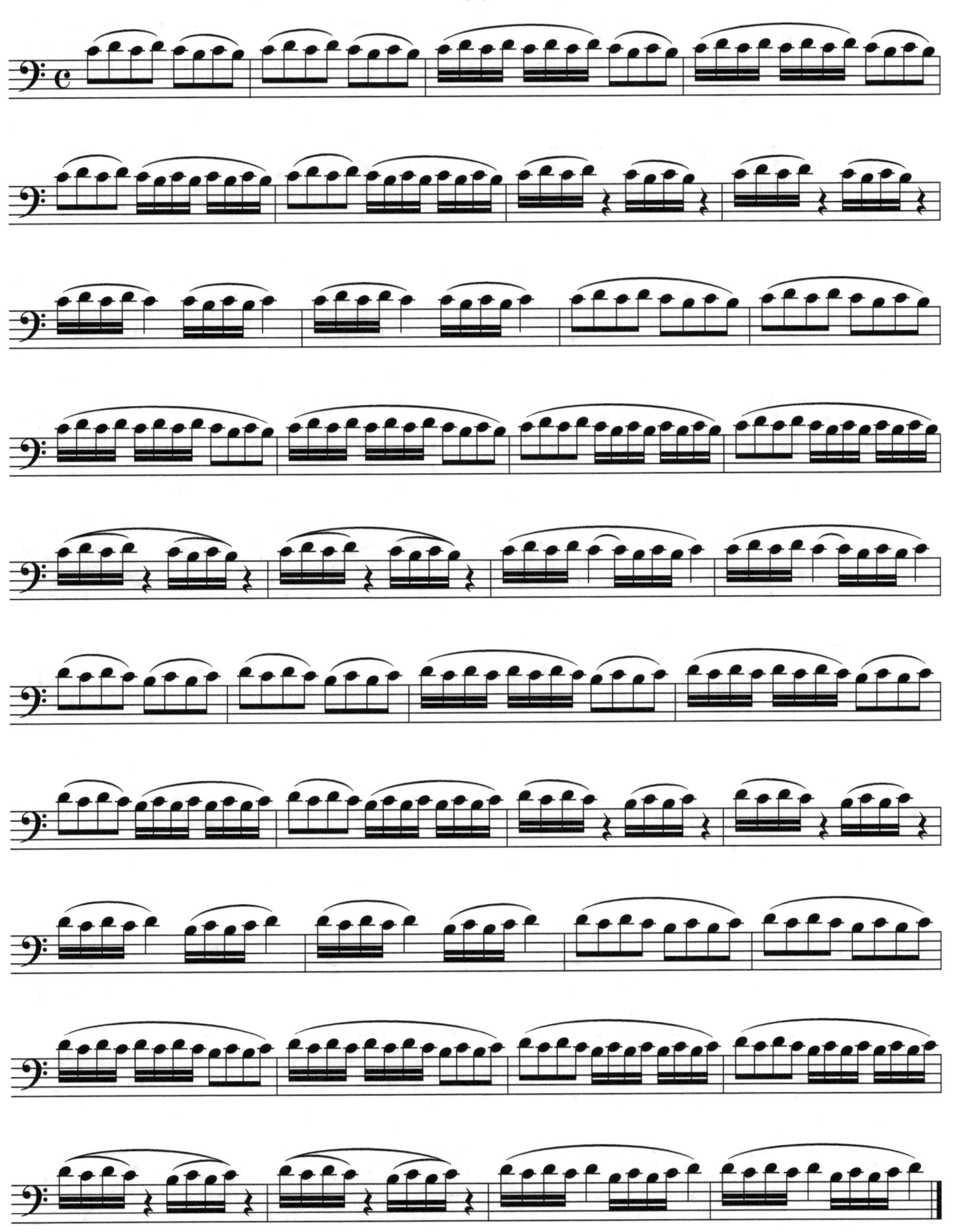

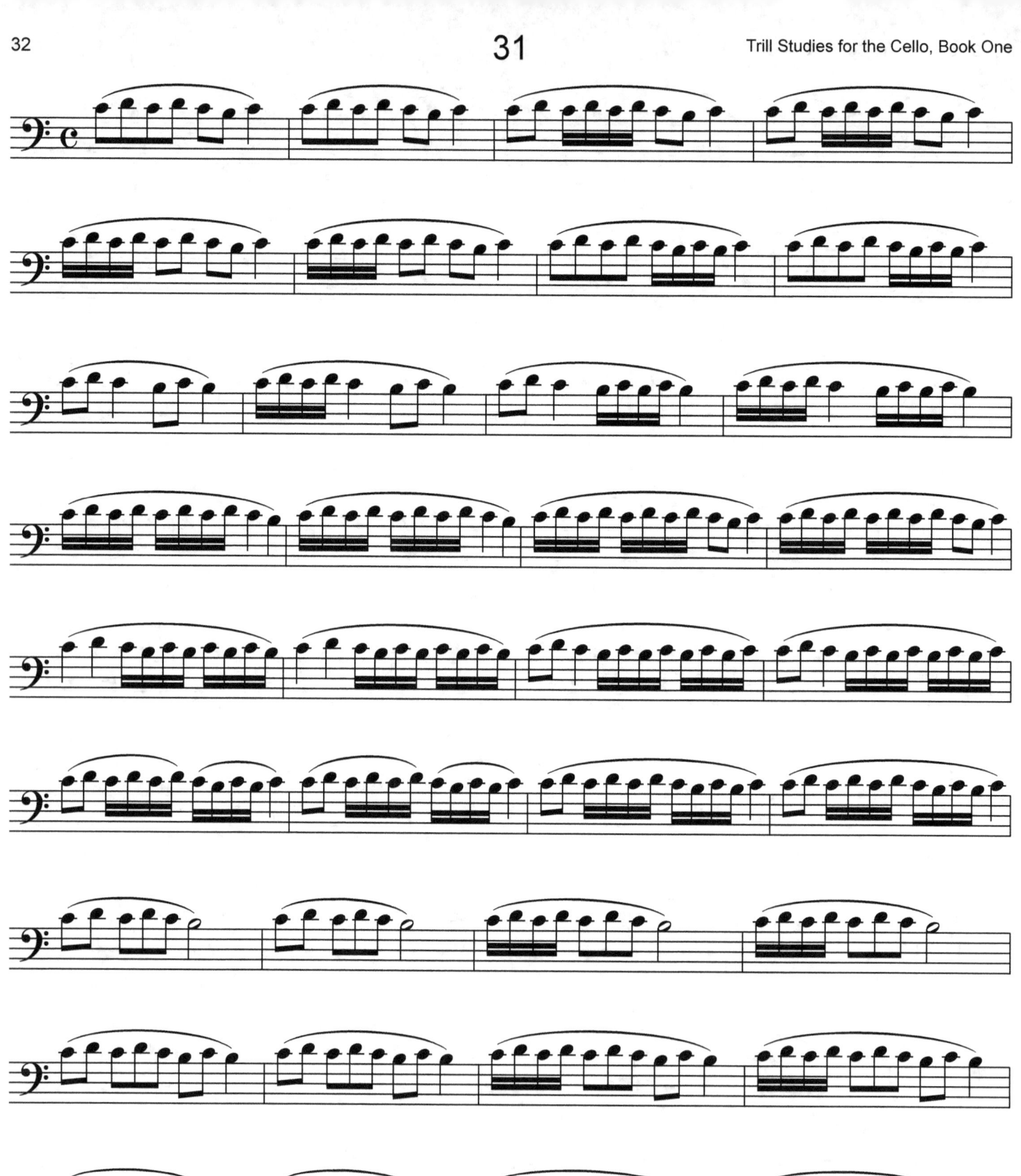

Trill Studies for the Cello, Book One

32

Trill Studies for the Cello, Book One

34

©2011 C. Harvey Publications All Rights Reserved.

Trill Studies for the Cello, Book One

36

©2011 C. Harvey Publications All Rights Reserved.

37

Trill Studies for the Cello, Book One

38

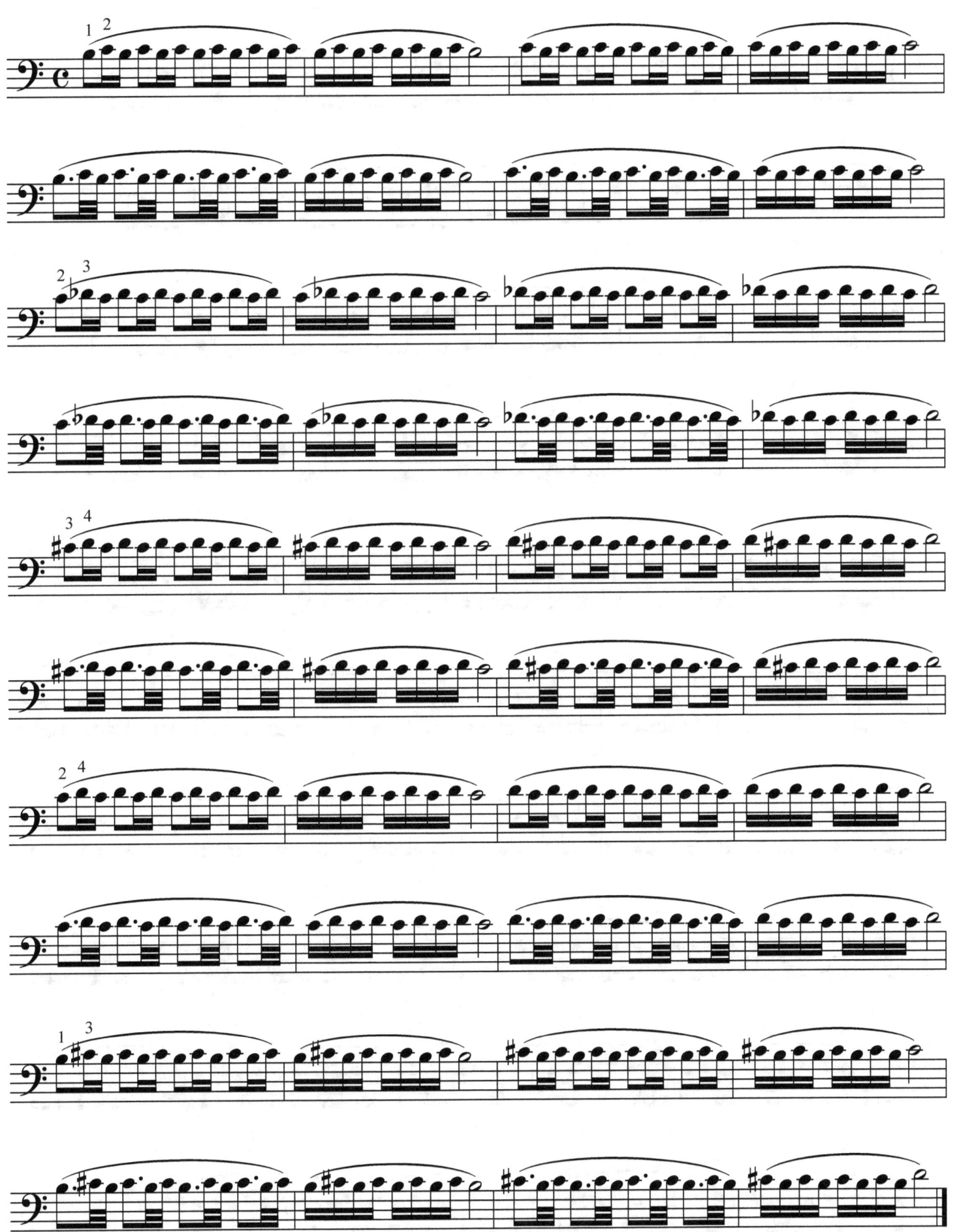

Trill Studies for the Cello, Book One

40

41

Trill Studies for the Cello, Book One

©2011 C. Harvey Publications All Rights Reserved.

Trill Studies for the Cello, Book One

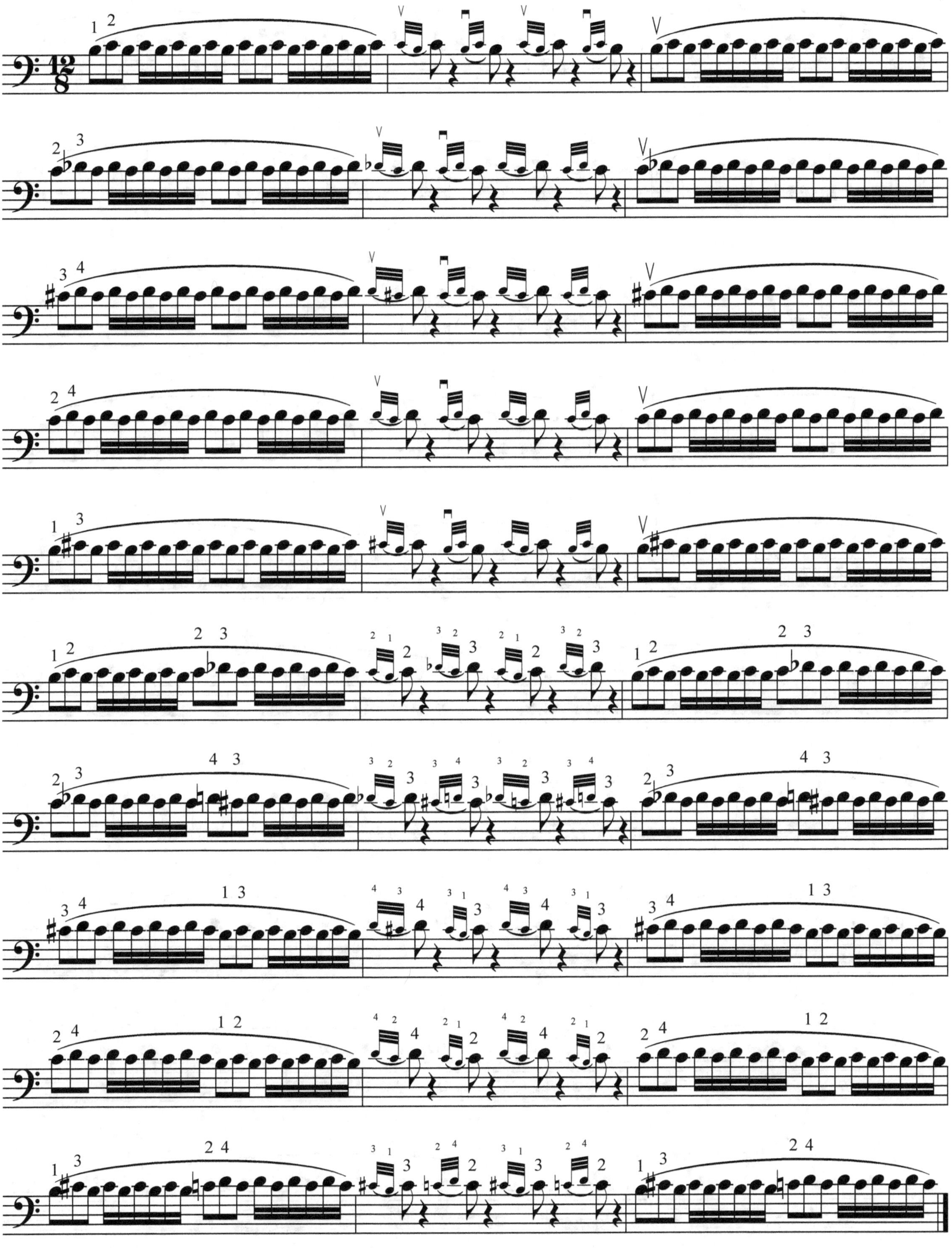

42

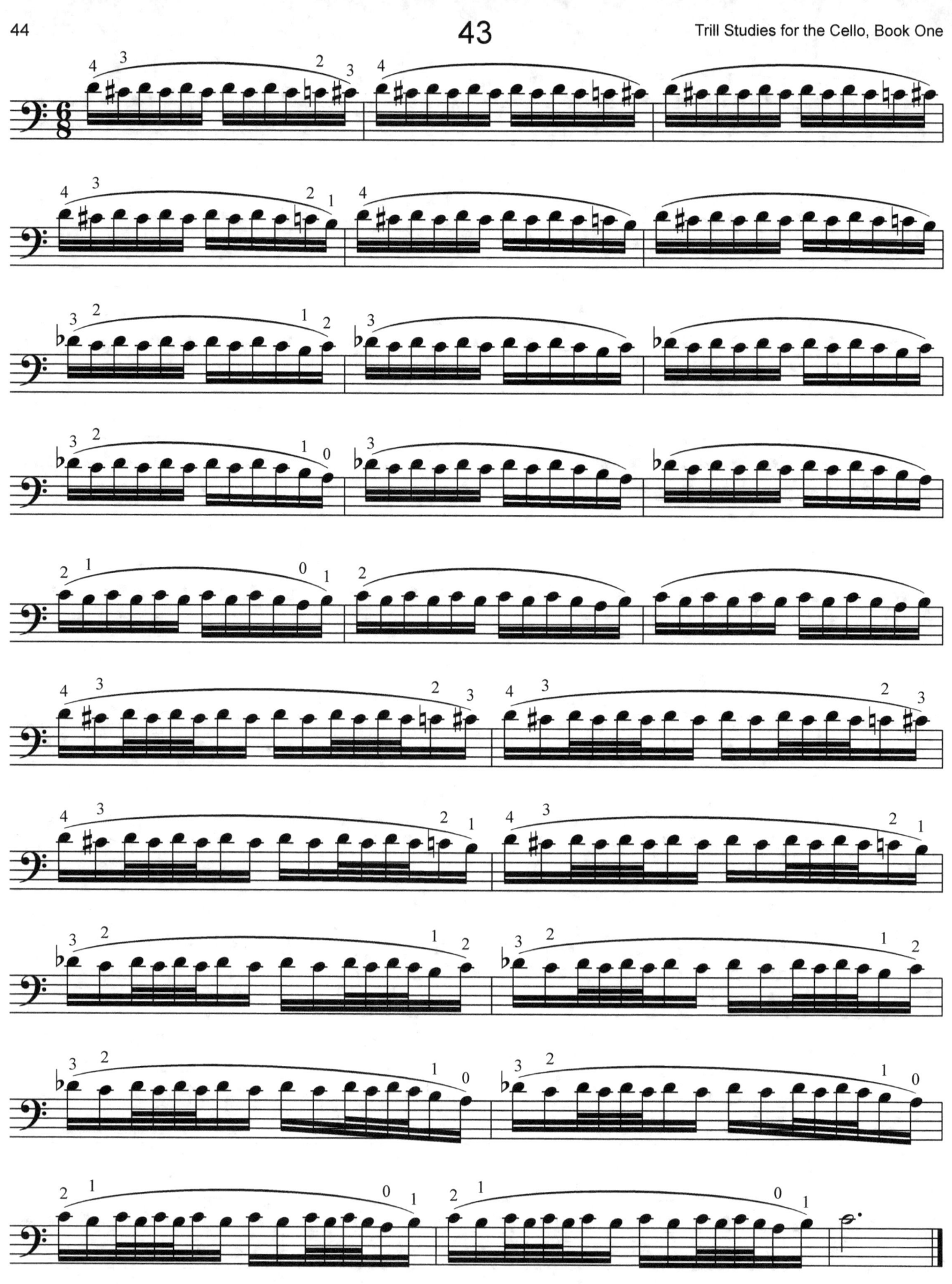

Trill Studies for the Cello, Book One

44

©2011 C. Harvey Publications All Rights Reserved.

available from **www.charveypublications.com**: CHP233

The Triplet Book for Cello, Part One

1

Left-Hand Warm-Up

Cassia Harvey

©2013 C. Harvey Publications All Rights Reserved.